# Annie's Gift

## Forward

As I set out to write this book about Man's best friend and my son I hope to embrace the reader with excitement as well as point out the value that a Dog can bring to one's life.  My intention is for this book to be one that will have an ongoing story so the reader will not only see the value but look forward to see how Annie's gift will help Ayden in the years to come.  Annie is a full blooded Yellow Lab that I rescued from someone that was going to dump her out at a landfill because their children wanted a new puppy.  Weather she has some sort of sixth sense to know I did this or not I don't know but she has been the most loyal dog I have ever had.  The story is based on true events with a little embellishment to bring strength and interest to the audience.  My prayer is that my readers will feel inspired knowing that if man's best friend can desire to help someone else how much more should we as humans do everything we can to help others. Annie my four legged best friend and my son has brought so much inspiration to my life.  With every faithful move of my Dog Annie to every smile on my son's face, to my faith in Christ, these are all things that bring encouragement and strength to me daily. They are always by my side weather I am working on my next project or sick in the bed they are there.  It reminds me of how God is.  He is always with us we just need to reach out and fill for him.

The sun was shining through the window of the old Farm House bedroom where Annie lay asleep on the bed. She always slept with her owner because she wanted to be close to him at all times. She is so loyal. She had earned her place on the family bed for being the most loyal dog he ever had. She stays by his side day and night no matter how many times he comes and goes she is always on his heels.

Having an owner that she could love and that loved her back, was something that Annie had longed for. She started her life with a family that didn't understand just how special she could be and decided they didn't want her. Annie came to live with the Crews family at age 3 and this was the best day of her life. From the very beginning she knew she had found an owner that would love her as much as she loved him. Not only was there Annie's new owner, but also 5 children and his wife to love her.

And love there is; it's like they were waiting on me or something. "I was treated so badly at my old home and now that I have been given a second chance at a great life I plan to make the most of it." "Some dogs might not understand this but when you've been where I have been you learn to appreciate the simple things in life thought Annie."

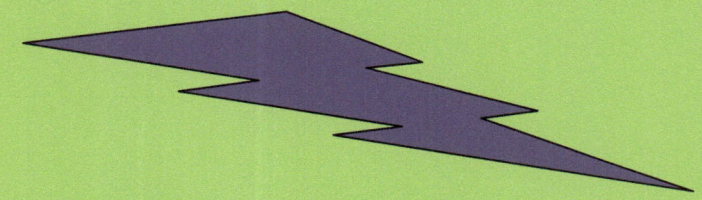

There are so many things I enjoy doing from swimming to playing ball, (ball being my favorite) but I also love spending time with my owners son Ayden. I get so excited when the ball comes out, but I quickly had to learn that excitement was something that had to be controlled when Ayden is around. He scares easily and he has a special need from birth that I realized required me to be on my best behavior.

Playing ball with my owner is my favorite past time. I have to stay on top of my game. I can chase the ball faster than any young whippersnapper could ever think.  See, I'm eight years old but I don't let that stop me. I'm a winner!!! I tell myself that because being positive always keeps my spirits up.  After all we are what we think, so I think I'm a winner!!!

Of course after a morning of chasing the ball and playing with my owner's son, Ayden, I do need a little rest on the couch. See, Ayden can't walk; he was born with Spina-Bifida. He is such a special little boy and I can see how much my owner loves him. I like to take the ball to him after running across the yard to fetch it. I always drop the ball a little ways from him and take my nose and push it to him. I don't want to take any chance of hurting him.

Ayden is so much fun. He probably doesn't realize it when he's watching other kids play and have fun, but for me he's a dream come true. He is always willing to play with me no matter what. I may be eight years old but I love to play and have fun. I have seen other little boys and girls with dogs like me that are pulling them in wheelchairs and picking up things for them. I wonder if I could do something like that for Ayden. I know it would make my human family happy if I could.

After all family helping family is what it's all about isn't it?  See, I guess I don't see myself as a dog but rather as part of the family.  My owner is the reason I feel this way. He has never made me feel like I was any less of a family member just because I walked on four legs instead of two.  I just wish there was something I could do to help Ayden.  He is so nice to me. He will throw my ball or play tug of war endlessly with me and I just want to do something for him.

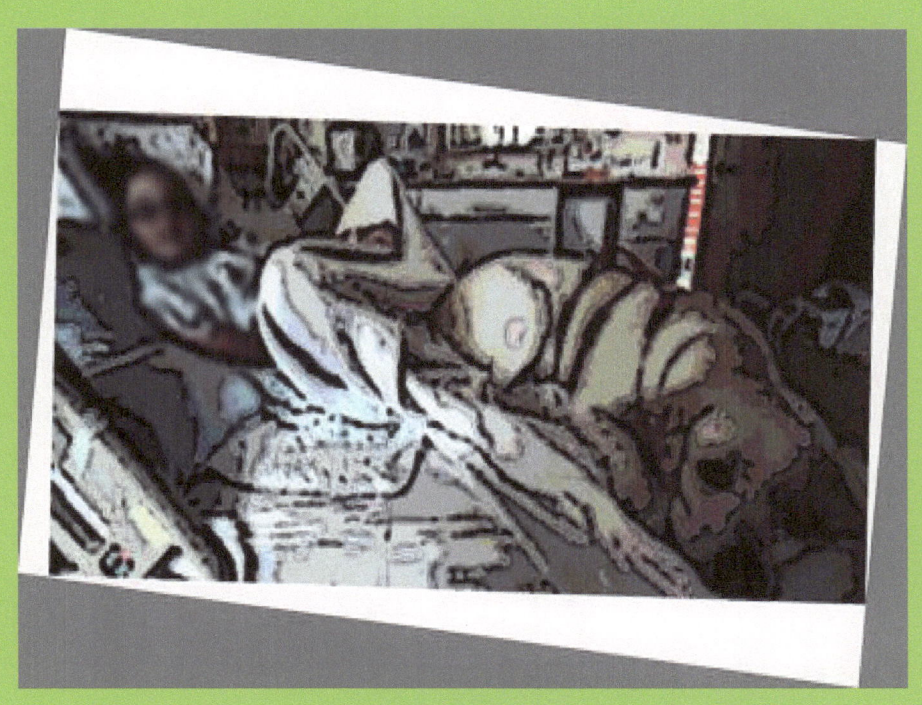

I overheard my human parents talking and it sounded like they were saying that it was time for Ayden to have another one of his surgeries. I've seen this before it seems like every few months they are gone for a couple of days. When they come back Ayden is all wrapped up in these white things with tape all over him. He cries some and sleeps a lot after he comes back from surgery, and I get very upset myself. I don't say anything but I like to stay really close. Since Ayden doesn't feel well his Dad and I lie on the bed with him for days on end. I don't mind because I know he doesn't feel well and he always makes time for me.

After a few days of rest it seems that things go back to normal around the Crews house hold. I dig out my old ball and get ready for some more fun. Now I know what you're thinking, all I do is want to chase a silly old ball right? No, that's not it at all I just want to have fun. It seems like my family wants the same thing. I still can't get the thought out of my head. How I wish I could do something more to help Ayden and the rest of my family. We do have a trip planned to town today. I think I'm going to get to go. I heard my owner asking where the sheet was at that he always puts over the car seat when I'm riding along. I don't want to ruin my image but I do shed a little. Maybe I can find something in town that can help me figure out what I can do for my family.

I was right! Road trip here we come!  I get so excited when I get to go anywhere.  I don't know what was planed today, but right now I'm just along for the ride.  I hope we get to go to that store that I get to go inside.  Most of the time I have to wait in the car while my family goes in and out of different places and sometimes we go to a store that I get to go inside.  Boy what fun it is, I get to see all sorts of things.  Big balls, little balls, soft balls, hard balls, rubber balls, cloth balls, ok, ok I know I'm stuck on the ball thing.  The first store I know we are going to is Wal-Mart.  No, I can't read but I've heard it talked about and had to wait in the car enough that I have figured out which store is Wal-Mart.  Wait, what is that I see, can it be, I have to be imaging things I know this can't be happening.

Yes it is exactly what I had seen once before. A
dog just like me walking with his owner right in
Wal-Mart. If their dog family can go in Wal-Mart
why can't I. I don't miss behave when I go in a
store. Well there was that one time that I lost all
my marbles and took off after a stray ball
bouncing across the floor but that was not at Wal-
Mart. So why does this boy get to take his dog in
but Ayden or my owner can't take me. I just don't
understand. I am going to get to the bottom of this
little matter I assure you. Now how am I going to
do that? I don't know how but I'm going to find
out something. I want to help Ayden like that dog
is helping his owner.

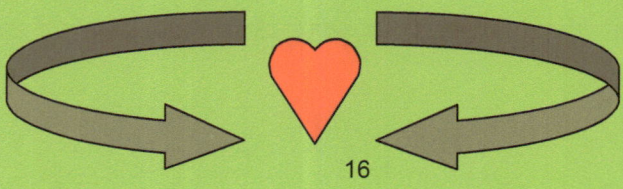

Well here comes my family with a cart full of goodies from Wal-Mart as usual. Maybe they have something for me. They walked right past the boy and his dog going in the store. Maybe, just maybe, they noticed the same thing I did. Just how come he can take this dog in Wal-Mart but they can't take me. If they noticed, then my job may be easier than I thought. See, I know my owner and the one thing I know about him is "if it's ok for one it's ok for all or no one should be allowed". So if they saw this I know he will be on the job finding out why I can't go in the store with them. Oh man, I was so hoping I could find a way to help Ayden on this trip. All I saw was another k-9 going where I can't go. All may not be lost though. I might be able to go in the store on the next trip.

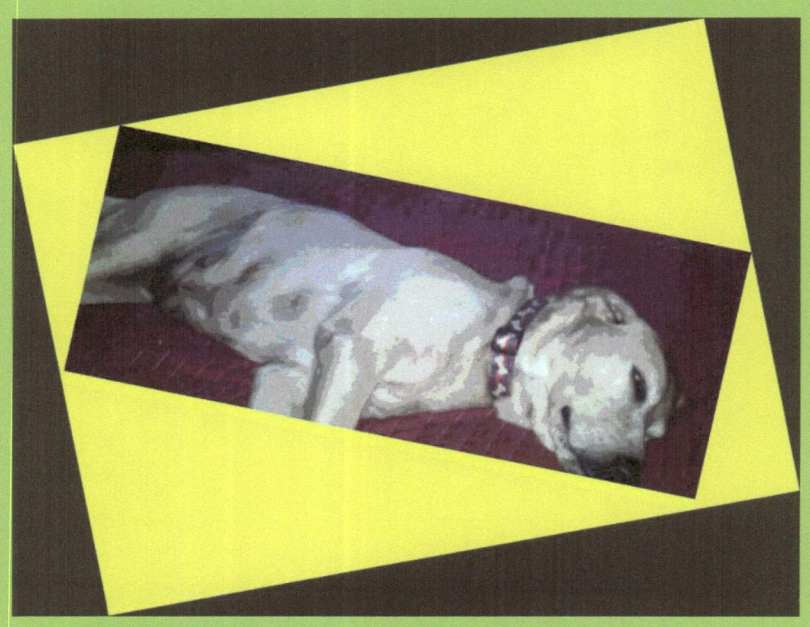

I guess my age shows doesn't it?  After a trip to town I do require a little rest. After all I'm eight years old and in human years that is equivalent to fifty-six years old.  So you can see why I feel the need to stretch out for a few hours for some zzzzzzzz's.  Maybe I can dream of my project. Oh, have you forgotten already? You know, how I can help my family more specifically the young Ayden.

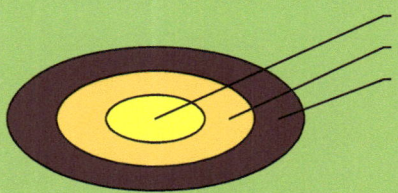

There that dog is again walking with his owner in Wal-Mart. Is this dajv'u, because I thought I already saw this? Oh wait a minute, I'm dreaming, there they go but what is this now I'm walking beside them. I'm helping the boy to pull his chair. Why am I dreaming about this? Maybe that's how I am supposed to help Ayden. But I don't think I can help him like this because I am just too old. After all, I give out of breath when I run a few times after my ball.

This is my dream and I'm so confused. What is this super natural force that seems to be guiding me through this dream?  That's right; I did say a prayer didn't I.  I know to pray because I hear my owner praying all the time.  I ask for God to show me how I can help.  This is the God that I always here my human family talking about.  I know that my owner is a Pastor because I go to the church with him when he goes to his office to study and pray.  I hear him calling out everyone's name to God asking him to protect them and help them to be closer to God.  That is what is happening to me; God has come to me in my dream and is helping me to know what I can do to help Ayden.

**Old Church building reminds me of God's blessings
both great and small.**

Now that is really weird. I see myself with a litter of puppies. I haven't had babies in many years.  As a matter of a fact, I think I'm too old to have a litter of puppies any more after all I am eight years old.  This is it though, I know now what God is showing me. I'm too old to help Ayden myself but if I can have babies again, just one more time, the puppy I give birth to can be trained to help Ayden.  That's my purpose! That is how I will be able to help my family.

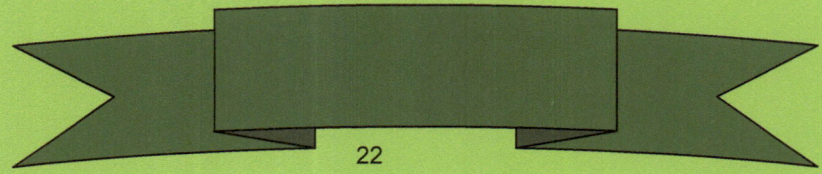

I can't believe it! I would have never thought it could be possible again. I am going to have babies! Finally, all the dreams, all the prayers of being able to help Ayden are going to come true.  I know God is going to allow me to have the perfect puppy for Ayden.  She will be his best friend just like I am for his Dad and she will be able to help him do things that he couldn't normally do by himself.  Thank you God for allowing me to be the one for this task.  I know you will give me the strength no matter what my age is. Amen

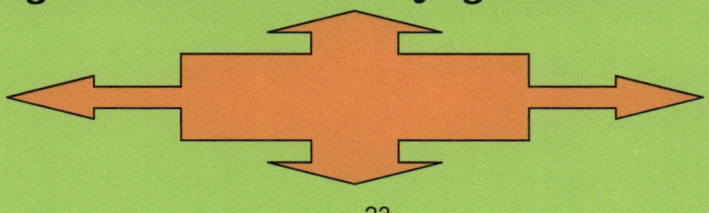

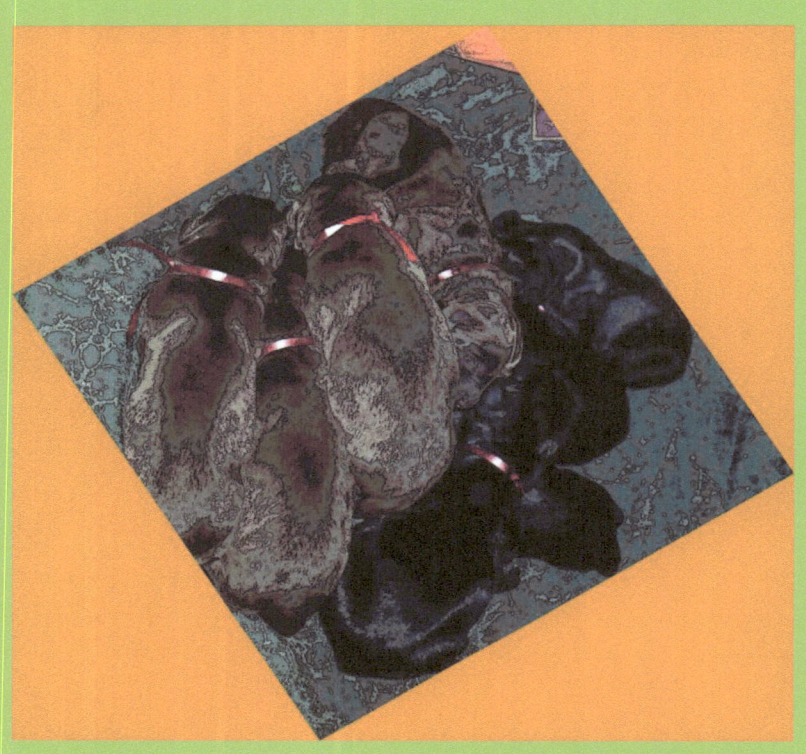

The day arrived! I had six boys and two girls four chocolate and four black.  The first born girl is the one for Ayden she will be a loyal companion for him for many years to come.  Ayden is so excited and has been for weeks anticipating the arrival of the puppies.  He has already named his puppy before she was ever born; I've heard him call her Zeva.  This time around has taken its toll on me, I'm very weak and this is definitely the last babies I will have.  God will give me strength.

Zeva is only eight weeks old now but soon she will embark on an adventure of a life time. Learning how to help Ayden with simple everyday tasks that most people take for granted. She will go through several weeks of training some with Ayden and some without but the most important part is he has a best friend for life.

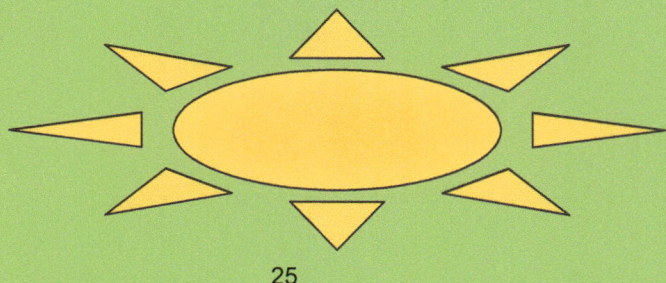

## Miscellaneous pictures of Annie and Ayden

# Continue miscellaneous pictures of Annie and Ayden

# Continue miscellaneous pictures of Annie and Ayden

28

# About the Author, Annie and Ayden

When I started this book "Annie's Gift" I really didn't know where it was going to end up. I really was writing just from the heart. Annie is a yellow lab that I rescued from a fellow employee that was going to put her out at a local land field (dump) because her children wanted a new puppy. They were given the choice by their parents to keep Annie or have a new puppy but not both. The employee's husband was literally on the way to the land field with Annie when we were having the conversation. I told her to call him immediately and tell him to bring her to the office and I would take her home with me. I couldn't stand the idea of any dog being dumped out not to mention she is full blooded. He brought her to me and that was the beginning of the best friendship I would ever have outside of my wife and children of course. Annie seemed to pick up on Ayden's disability right away. It was amazing to watch her when being around him. She always used such careful movements and precise maneuvers to ensure to not hurt him or upset him. When he got his first wheel chair she would pull him in it without any training whatsoever. We realized just how much a service dog could help Ayden. With Annie being eight years old we knew she was too old to invest the money it would take to fully train her to help him and her loyalty really lied more with me than with Ayden. So we made the decision to let her have puppies in hopes of having one that would have the same disposition as Annie for Ayden. After careful consideration and a complete checkup with our veterinarian our plan worked wonderfully, Annie had eight puppies with two being female. The first born is the one that we decided would be the best for Ayden as a service dog. The puppy is only ten weeks old at the completion of this book but we plan on sending her for training very soon.

www.ingramcontent.com/pod-product-compliance
Lightning Source LLC
Chambersburg PA
CBHW050911290526
45792CB00002B/776